GUTENBERG IN STRASBOURG

OTHER BOOKS BY ROSALIE MOORE

The Grasshopper's Man & Other Poems, Yale University Press, 1949.

The Year of the Children: Poems for a Narrative of the Children's Crusade in Europe in 1212 A.D., Woolmer/Brotherson Publishers, 1977.

Of Singles and Doubles, Woolmer/Brotherson Publishers, 1979.

Gutenberg
in Strasbourg

Rosalie Moore

FLOATING ISLAND PUBLICATIONS

CEDARVILLE / CALIFORNIA
1995

ISBN: 0-912449-52-7

Published by:
Floating Island Publications
P.O. Box 341
Cedarville, CA 96104

ACKNOWLEDGEMENTS

Thanks to a group of artists calling themselves The Eggotists
who, led by Elizabeth Berryhill, were the first to see this
manuscript through its many stages. Special gratitude to
Marjorie Casebier McCoy and Charles Sherwood McCoy who
revealed to me Germany, both sides of the wall, and the
Gutenberg Museum at Mainz.

Particular heartfelt thanks to the many friends and supporters—
led by Gerald Fleming, Barbara Swift Brauer, Diana O'Hehir,
Jean Pumphrey, Kay Ryan, and others—who made the
publication of *Gutenberg in Strasbourg* possible.

Special thanks to Deborah Turrietta, calligrapher, for personal
and historical insights into the art of writing.

To the memory of my parents,
Marvin Moore and Teresa Wooldridge Moore;
and to the belief and inspiration of Peter Sharkey.

TABLE OF CONTENTS

NOTES ON A BEGINNING

Rosalie insists it was conversations among us, especially with our students, which evoked the book at hand. It began thirty years ago when three of us came together to help establish a Communications Department at College of Marin. We were Maryjane Dunstan, Chairman, who was to introduce Future Studies at the College; myself—a student of languages who had been teaching Russian as well as English with the help of the new technology; and Rosalie Moore, a poet and musician who had been an early radio writer. We drew in others: Judy Gartman, David Newby, Dyan Pike, to add perspectives on film, TV, computers and other media. Paul Miller gave us a Biblical dimension. We were lucky to have Rosalie who knew what metaphors can do right from the beginning. Later, another poet, Kay Ryan. Because Metaphor is a catalyst for catapulting us from a familiar location into another imagined or foreseen. Of course we hooked on to Marshall McLuhan, the English professor who forced us to observe with Joycean freshness the procession of contemporary developments: his images made sense of the real—made senses reel.

Gutenberg's revolution, which took place in the middle of the fifteenth century made senses reel as ours do today under the revolution of modern media. One thing we were learning in our consideration of the mass media is that people in the throes of media change—from period to period—all act and react in very much the same way.

Now, thirty years later, Rosalie Moore has written this book which illuminates Gutenberg's revolution, so much like our own. And yet, while this poem is the story of the inventor of the Secret Art, the inner life of the writer makes art for us. We owe it all to Gutenberg who made it possible for us to read these hand-crafted words that the poet's imagination sets down for eyes and ears—no, for all our senses—to reel in.

As the narrator says when discussions began to fly, "And concepts raged like bees."

—Jack de Benedictis

PROLOGUE

Monks & Troubadours

Many inventors had been working for a number of years to discover ways to make "Artificial Writing," as they called it, feasible. When the production of Gutenberg's Bible in 1450 made the possibility a reality, there was a universal upheaval. Not only would calligraphers be out of work, but the Gospel could then be spread indiscriminately among people who were not prepared to receive it. All manner of myth and unfit story and information would be available for the ignorant and vulnerable throughout the world.

A Monastic Scriptorium

THE MASTER COPYIST IN A MONASTERY AT MT. CENIS, IN
THE ALPS, PROTESTS THE INVENTION OF PRINT. HE
WARNS CALLIGRAPHERS OF THE WORLD TO UNITE
AGAINST PRINTERS.

Prophecy: 1450

For well I know . . . (too soon!) . . . that Print
                    my Devil
Will come by a narrow door—
Clamp down with sevenfold malediction
                    of Vaticans
To foul all Scripture with his vampire's
                    bite.

Christ on his cross is not so sad a spectacle
As language misused, cramped and enslaved
In iron moulds and made to serve churls.

Now prophets no longer range through the
                    testament hills,
Nor apples appear with serpents, true
                    in their colors:
Illumination is ended! The viscous smell
                    of ink on pulp
Revolts me! I see the heavens all clogged
                    with papers—
Billowing, endless: not clouds, but
                    dirty paragraphs of weather—
Each blocking the view of the last in
                    emended editions!—
And all of the trees of the universe gone
                    like martyrs.

For they shall crack the looms for fuel,
                              the tapestries rend
And masticate the linens for pulp and
                              power.
In the end, no animal shall wear his skin,
No tree his heart, no man his countenance.

In my day we gave scripture colors, and
                              eye-resting fields.
A Saint could speak from the column
                              of an "I."
Samson swelling his muscles fit in an "X,"
While vile Holofernes slept in the tent
                              of an "A."
I liked to reserve the letter "V" for the
                              Virgin,
Or under the boughs of a "T" to begin
                              a psalm.
I return to my manuscript; I say
                              nothing more.
I care for the Word. Let God take care
                              of the Printers.

IN AN AUGUSTINIAN MONASTERY NEAR MAINZ COPYISTS
ALSO HAVE FOREWARNINGS OF THE ADVENT OF PRINT. THEY
HEAR RUMBLINGS IN THE EARTH AND IN THE STOMACH. NOW
THAT THE PLAGUE HAS SUBSIDED, SOME EXPECT FURTHER
ABOMINATIONS AS PREDICTED IN THE APOCALYPSE. OTHERS,
LIKE ALBERTUS, WAIT FOR LIFE TO REVEAL ITSELF.

Brother Albertus, the Kindly—a Scribe

In the scriptorium, he leans to his
high slant board. The hearth well-tended,
no chill air enters his stomach
in stone-warmed halls.

Fat at his bench, on his buttocks
of honor and pride, he writes
in his guiltless white the words
from God—in parchment clear,
each page a countryside, and
full of the sounds of the sea.

When his Brothers sidle past
to glimpse his work, he flushes
with admiration of his Capitals.
He could make letters
capital or common. He is not
a specialist like Everettdig,
and thus of more use to God.

Brother Everettdig puts in
the umlauts
over the vowels.

Albertus is devout,
and sparkles with gossip.
He keeps his stomach full
as balance and prop.

His dreams by night
are the same as his thoughts
by day. He does not have
to monitor his conscience—
the Scriptures enfold them all:
work, prayers, digestion.
May the tides recant and cease
if he thinks of else.

He eats only the whites of eggs,
having heard in the village
that the yolk sometimes conceals
an illicit seed.

This was told him
by Corsican sailors,[1] spicy
and evil. They were on their way
to Rome to buy indulgences
and change their way of life,
having left their ships.
And talking to these gave him
something to confess.
This happened near
the communal latrine,
in Middle Day, at the time
when the bird-songs cease.

Now he hears the bells
for Matins. Taking his bulk
to the chapel, he sits by
Everettdig on stony benches.

---

1. These are gypsies, who by now have stolen his draw-string purse.

Albertus's true owl, Simonides,
winks from the rafters.
Simonides lives in the belfry
overhead, but flies
when the great bell swings.

HYSTERIA OVER PRINTING IS SPREADING IN EPIDEMIC PROPORTIONS. THE CLERGY IN SOME AREAS BELIEVE THE POPE SHOULD BAN ALL DOCUMENTS PRODUCED BY MECHANICAL MEANS. ARTIFICIAL WRITING IS ESPECIALLY DEPLORED BY COPYISTS, AS PRINTERS' DEVILS RUN THROUGH THE STREETS DELIVERING COMPLETED VOLUMES TO RICH PATRONS.

Brother Everettdig the Gloomy, Calligrapher's Helper

"The printers are sending their
devils through Christendom
uprooting flowers for hashish
on which they feed—chewing
on poppies and milkweed,
ruining souls.
                    "I keep my demon
within, where he ruins no one,
though he causes foul sounds
and other indelicacies.

"If I were lessoned to draw,
as Albertus is, I would make
capitals ample as widows gravid
and swelling with love for me.

"Like such a woman, I give
a being home, that there
might be one less evil
creature about and roaming.

"Holy men labor to discover God's design:
some look to bird flights,
others watch cloud formations.
I forward the science of prophecy
studying entrails of bill-pointing
grebes and chickens.

"Now the printers
gather in guild-halls and use
Black Arts. Their coffers are
filled with gold, for they
melt down chalices, use ink
for the blood of Christ.

"Later they take their books
to profane fairs where sons
of princes buy them, who love
to read about fornication
among the ancients."

The story of a miracle is told:
A Doge of Venice received
a commissioned volume, mouth
set for a meal of reading.
But when he looked, the words
had fled the page; no mark
of the metal's bite on
the virginal parchment. The noble
visage opened: lips, beard,
and jowls, and the Doge
stared, with the mouth
of a hungry lion.

IN A UNIVERSE WHERE COMMUNICATION THROUGH
SOUND—INCLUDING THAT OF THE HUMAN VOICE—WAS
PARAMOUNT, MINNESINGERS AND TROUVÈRES GAVE
INSPIRATION AND SOLACE. SOME, LIKE FRANÇOIS VILLON,
LIVED ON INTO THE ERA OF PRINTING.

The Troubadour

— O ring from which the ruby is out-falle[2]

People were used to listening
to what they heard: were it bee
in its midnight of sun
or consummate bell . . . its circles
slowly widening the air . . .
each hears in his own
vernacular and resolve
the creak and stretch
of leather on a stair.

The storyteller casts his
fisher's net as on a lake,
brings home a hive of lights;
brings towers and banners home,
and ladies lovely as goldfish
flashing in waters,
and chivalry—all sung
by the gifted singer, airy
and fine in his sleeves.

---

2. Chaucer, *Troilus and Crisseyde*

But now the words are
separate from the song:
no pucker of lute nor
mandolin's nip and tuck,
no power to hold at ease
the fisted heart.

Sun-drenched and alone
the Troubadour awakes
on a slanting beach,
to tell the waves what
belongs to the sea already . . .

Calligraphy, our necessary
life from hand to hand,
becomes an Art, is often
under glass . . . and words
unsettled without music.

The Troubadour is asked
to furnish proof of his
stories of Troy or Carthage:
this he cannot give—himself
the Fool-proof wanderer—saying
"I have 'lied' to you many times,
in song, in love, in Truth."

THE ARCHBISHOP OF MAINZ SPEAKS ONCE A MONTH TO
THE MONKS FROM THE MONASTERY, THE DATE VARYING
BECAUSE IT IS CHOSEN BY THE SAME PROCEDURE
FOLLOWED TO DETERMINE THE DATE OF EASTER IN THE
ECCLESIASTICAL CALENDAR. THE BROTHERS ARE USED
TO HEARING MASS IN THEIR SMALL STONE CHAPEL. NOW
THEY ENTER THE MOST PRESTIGIOUS CHURCH IN THE
RHINELAND PALATINATE. VARIOUS AND SUNDRY PERSONS
COME INTO THE CATHEDRAL FROM OFF THE STREETS TO
JOIN THE CONGREGATIONS. THE ARCHBISHOP IS KNOWN
TO BE AN "ENLIGHTENED" PONTIFF, AN ADMIRER OF
HILDEGARD OF BINGEN.[3]

His Holiness, The Archbishop

Carrying himself this way and that
through bits of metal and glass—
embroideries to turn the heads
of angels—the Archbishop himself
says Mass, lest the Brothers forget
he is the ruling prelate.
Albertus and Everettdig arrive
through the flocking air, enter
through common gates where stone-
cutters come, or mimes, or churls
with paint on their aprons: any
with bunion on foot or lame
with a curse; or heretic may come
through unguarded doors.

---

3. Hildegard of Bingen: A twelfth century saint, an Abbess, naturalist,
   and early holistic thinker.

High on a wall there is Latin
in glistening granite which few
can read, Albertus one of the few.
The edges of objects surprise him—
gold-rimmed chalices, shining
communion plate, the candles swaying
in councils of seven or five.
He feels nauseated. Everettdig
tells him the cathedral
is a bower pagan with flowers.
The Brothers decide they should
not take Communion.

The Archbishop is Master of Ritual
and Thinker for his flock. When
he turns, a tree of lightnings
showers above him. He is present
in his appearance, and disappearance.
In the Cathedral, the people blossom.
He lightens their lives
with flickers of rubies and diamonds.

He reads the Gospel in Latin
for the contented. Now, with
a quarter-turn, he gives the Bible
to altar-boys in white
who tip with its weight.

(The Gutenberg, when it comes,
is heavier still: two volumes
treasured in cedar.)
                    The Archbishop
speaks of this event, a sermon
beginning. The ribands fall,
without frivolity, from his
yellow cassock, in this
post-Easter season. He is

blessing the printers "and all
holy Craftsmen" who will
bring us the Word, though in
new and mysterious forms.

Albertus lunges, then holds
to the sturdy pews. Closing
his eyes, he sees colors
of violet and puce.
                      Albertus,
the Terrified now, remembers
Evil. The Archbishop allows
the Feast of the Asses[4] to rage—
this on Fat Tuesday. And also
in Lenten season, with common
jesters, he laughs at
the Feast of the Fools.[5]

Closed as a turtle, and bent
with the sins of others, Brother Albertus
leaves the tainted Cathedral.
Everettdig follows,
cursing the time of year.

---

4. Feast of Asses: a ceremony ridiculing the Mass, considered by some
   to be therapeutic.

5. Feast of Fools: a similar celebration in which Fools are allowed to
   rule for a day.

Albertus and Everettdig Return to the Monastery

They enter the cloister,
passing the gardener's kingdom.
Everettdig says gardens
are only battle-grounds
where lilies immortal cavort
with foul leeks, and where
evil weeds—extracted—
keep coming back.

Albertus notices only
the passing wafts,
and odors delicious as
having two bowls of whey.
Relief at escaping from
the venal Cathedral
sharpens both his
confusion and observation.

The year is green, the grass
comes toward him an inch.
Even as Everettdig tells him
the horrors of hell, a fresh
and upstart, newborn lily
greets him.
                    He thinks how
the common daylight is falling
everywhere to the ground,
and he wishes he could make love
in the country air.

                    He calls down Simonides, his owl,
to help him tarry; but Simonides
only wants to hunt and fly.

His life indoors awaits him,
safe as a shadow. Albertus
will enter capitals
on new velum, some round as melons,
some winding like Arabic scarves.

IN AUGUST DEVOUT CALLIGRAPHERS START PREPARING
SCHEDULES AND SPECIAL SERVICES FOR THE FOLLOWING
RELIGIOUS YEAR. ALTHOUGH THE ECCLESIASTICAL
CALENDAR IS IN GENERAL USE IN MOST ORDERS IN
GERMANY, THE AUGUSTINIAN MONASTERY NEAR MAINZ
LONG AGO ADOPTED A CALENDAR ESTABLISHED IN 46 B.C.
BY JULIUS CAESAR. POPE GREGORY THE GREAT WOULD
NOT BE HERE ON EARTH TO INTEGRATE BOTH CALENDARS
UNTIL 1582.

Brother Albertus the Kindly: The Book of Hours

While others are writing responses
for High Masses, schedules for
kitchen or chapel, rules and reminders,
Albertus tries to finish
a Book of Hours, arranged by his
Abbot, for the Doge of Venice.

He picks up a sturdier quill
for an Initial.
           After Albertus,
the rubricator will come to fill
the letter with clear and living
scarlet.
        The Monks in charge
of abbreviations come, to provide
the usual symbols. They are
specialists, and bring their own
ink and quills.
           (Albertus is sad:
he will soon not see again
his Book of Hours.)
           Its last
adornment, gold from floating
sheets, reflects the sun.

Illumination is light
to that Century,
and the book, its flower.

Gutenberg knew calligraphy
and tried to save its art.
His readers would say,
"You can hardly
tell the difference."

In the scriptorium monks
who were working on schedules
hoped that His Eminence
would not forbid them
their usual Julian calendar.

From Dante they knew that
Caesar's shade was languishing
somewhere in limbo. He died
before Jesus' time, so
some of the fervid decided
to pray for his shivering soul.

GUTENBERG IN MAINZ

Profits & Alchemists

CRAFTSMEN EVERYWHERE WERE GATHERING TO
FORMULATE THEIR RIGHTS AND DEMANDS. JOHANN
WANTS TO JOIN THE GOLDSMITHS' GUILD BUT WAS
BARRED BECAUSE OF HIS FAMILY CONNECTIONS. HE
COULD NOT, THEREFORE, PURCHASE HIS NEEDED METALS:
ONE OF HIS CRAFTSMEN FRIENDS HAD TO DO IT FOR HIM.
STYLES IN JEWELRY AND OTHER FINE METAL OBJECTS,
PROFANE AND SACRED, WERE CHANGING RAPIDLY.

Unrest was everywhere. It was
in the air. Tradesmen in Dusseldorf
dreamed of more rapid transit
in sharp-keeled boats speeding
southward to Cologne. In Italy
upstart Dukes with profiles
on local silver were carried
from hand to hand; became legal
tender, tossing aside some Emperor.
Blowers of glass blew worlds inside
of worlds, each one with Venetian
colors. Even the pounders,
installers of pipes and fountains
listened and heard: an intricate
rising of rivers was in their ears.

In Germany ladies and courtiers
alike were tired of looking into
the bald, flat eyes of medieval
stones. Vast necklaces and brooches
had become unmanageable—even by
Kings and Queens whose aching
muscles held in place the signs
of wealth and lineage they lived by.

Artisans themselves worked with
a fury of Goths to find new ways
to bring fires into garnets,
again make amethysts lovely.
Masters of lights that flash
out of rubies and diamonds,
they saw themselves as the curers
of the malaise, the doctors of
the dallying arts.
      Johann wasn't
with them. Aslant of connections,
he never joined the goldsmiths.
His dogged but much loved experiments
began: in seven years he would be
melting Alsatian copper into his ink
to make it cling to metal.
His hands kept ready,
skill socketed into the bone—
his mind retooling
to a different purpose.

THE CITY MINT AT MAINZ WAS FOUNDED BY PETER
GENSFLEISCH—GRANDPA PETERKIN—WHOSE DESCENDANTS
CONTINUED TO RUN IT. ONE GREAT GRANDSON IS
SOMETHING OF A PROBLEM. HE LIKES TO EXPERIMENT
WITH METALS AND MAKE COINS OF UNUSUAL SHAPES.

Johann Gensfleisch[6] zum Gutenberg (1400-1468)

On a bench before him
were silver and gold in packets
for coins in differing weights
and sizes. To his left, Grandfather
in profile—that gifted ghost,
whose statue stood near the entrance.
Though dead for years, he was silver
to Johann's carbon.[7] The two
ignited each other.

No one was better than Johann
at striking coins or melding
congenial metals or making moulds.
He often would stay at the Mint
all day while his relatives
were out collecting rents,
at Burghers' meetings,[8]

---

6. Gensfleisch is the family name; it means "gooseflesh." Gutenberg is
   a place, the name of the family estate.

7. Carbon: "A naturally abundant non-metallic element that occurs in
   all organic compounds and is capable of chemical self-bonding to
   form an enormous number of chemical biologically or commercially
   important long-chain molecules" (*American Heritage Dictionary*).

8. Gutenberg's father was one of five city council members who
   presided over the city. He is not mentioned in any accounts I have
   access to, and may have died before events, here recorded, began.

or blowing the foam from a stein
to their City's pride.

When Johann left, he would visit
with Alchemists, or pore over
Latin scrolls with Father Heilmann . . .
But even more than the scrolls—
since he was seven—Johann had
loved a book alive with colors,
made by an unknown scrivener.

        Father Heilmann
let Johann hold it, turning
page after glorious page.
What stained glass had inspired
in an earlier time was now
invoked by books—and you could
own one; but that would require
the cost of two fine horses.

"A study for priests and scribes."
The relatives shook their heads.
"And on top of that, he wants
to be a goldsmith."

Farther back in the Mint
in the clattering half-dark
was Freile, half-brother to Johann—
Asthmatic, he was older—but still
an adequate wielder of iron.

His copper face seemed always
looking straight forward,
his ears attuned to the passing
of horses' hooves. He was thinking
how many horseshoes he could make—
were it not for the City mint—
how many good tapering axes.

Whenever the moon was full
and flat as a guilder,
Johann would think, *"There's
a coin to buy the world with."*
He liked the moon with its face
that looked directly, for
people on coins had profiles
that turned away.

The metals Johann worked with
came out of the secretive earth.
But here was a silver of a higher order . . .

Some people felt a shift.
It was just before the birth
of Copernicus.
              This thin
pancake of a world was
flat then, Columbus not yet
rounding his corner,
and a thousand questions were
lurking behind Church pillars.
Avoiding the indefinite,
Johann decided to make himself
Master of Metals.

He stamps out another coin.

The Alchemist

THE ALCHEMISTS CULTIVATED MANDRAKES AND
CHAMELEONS AND WERE SAID SOMETIMES TO OWN PIECES
OF RHINOCEROS HORN. THEIR INFLUENCE FLOURISHED
TO ENLIGHTEN, AND TO BEFOG—ESPECIALLY IN ZURICH,
THE BIRTHPLACE OF PARACELSUS. ONE OF THEIR NUMBER,
NOSTRADAMUS, PREDICTED THE APPEARANCE OF ANOTHER
GREAT DOCTOR WHO—IN A FAR DISTANT TIME, WOULD
PROCLAIM THEIR WISDOM AND UPON IT BASE A WHOLE
NEW SCIENCE OF SELF-KNOWLEDGE.[9]

The Alchemists I.

Impatient with their meetings
roaring with silence—
the silence of Found Men—
and unable to add his cubit—

Johann, preoccupied—in their
opinion—with future profits,
asked question after question
about metals: their weights,
uses, and valences, their price.

About silence, the Alchemists said
they were used to each other;
they would speak when they got ready.
When they did, they quoted Jabir
and Paracelsus. They learned
about prime matter from Aristotle—
but that could be changed by fire,
by concentration, by addition
of marvelous elements they knew.

---

9. Not until the 20th century did Carl Gustav Jung rediscover the
   work of the Alchemists and use it as a model for psychotherapy.

In truth, the ancient gods came out
to watch, like scavengers empty
of sack . . . for now the Alchemists
were their own creators.

                They smiled
when they said it. Perhaps
they added themselves
to the formula:
the life, the experiment.

The Alchemists II.

"The experiment has been boiling
long enough." He told his Alchemist
friends, "I *have* the gold. What
I need is the lead you keep
turning to something else."

Goodbye to the Alchemists,
those stirrers of cauldrons—
the acrid smells, the fires'
endless muttering. Without mirrors,
they see their faces in their
spoons, their myriad colors
reflected in those faces.

Later they drop
the Arabic "Al"—to become
the Chemists of a future time.

All science begins with a mystical
devotion that continues after
the lung-diving work is over.
It continues by ritual,
by people like Peter Schoeffer—
Gutenberg's prime assistant—
by imitation. Change, that insult,
is accepted or forgotten,
and again people sing, or sleep . . .

Gutenberg did neither:
became inventor,
lived to see the day . . .
thought of the Alchemists.

WITH SO MANY PEOPLE NOW MOVED OUTSIDE OF CASTLE WALLS, MORE SMALL MERCHANTS OF GOODS AND SERVICES WERE APPEARING: SOME IN THE CITY MARKETS, SOME WITH THEIR WARES ON THE BACKS OF OXEN OR DONKEYS, SOME AT THE WALLS OF A CATHEDRAL. BY 1430 THE FIRM OF FUST AND GUTENBERG OFFERED SHELTER TO BUYERS. IN A FINE LARGE WORKSHOP REPLETE WITH TOOLS AND PACKAGES THEY SOLD ETCHINGS, LITHOGRAPHS, AND PLAYING CARDS, AS WELL AS WOODBLOCK PRINTS FOR ALL OCCASIONS.

The Firm of Johann zum Gutenberg and Johannes Fust

After all, Johann had his own
kind of magic: he could read words
backwards more quickly than a wood-
pecker moving and dancing, or make
a whole page woodblock for a pamphlet:
he didn't sit down very much—he had
three things going. He could make stones
speak, when he made a lithograph;
and he had learned calligraphy
from Father Heilmann.

When he cut a woodblock, he wrote
in a backwards language. Pressed
on a paper, it turned into good
High German. Some people thought
this was dangerous: it was rumored
that Holy Mass, said backwards,
gave power to witches.

                    Johann's partner
was Johannes Fust, an advocate,
with money to invest in promising
endeavors. He didn't know
what this particular Gensfleisch

was up to; Johann was different
from the rest, and had enormous
talents. Now that he made
a woodblock better than others,
he planned to abandon wood
and make blocks with metal.
He said wood splintered.
Fust wouldn't care, so long as
he received his reimbursement.

Johann made bracelets and rings
in metals that Fust could purchase.
Himself not a goldsmith,
Fust still knew the uses of gold.

The partners had an assistant,
one Peter Schoeffer, only twenty,
perhaps, to Johann Gensfleisch's
thirty. Without peer as an aide,
handsome, ingratiating,
he could imitate perfectly
any performance of Johann's.
So Johann's hands were then
to be Peter's hands, when—banished,
the Gensfleisch went elsewhere,
two of them to Strasbourg.

But then there would be something
to come back to, for the third
son of Freile and Else Gensfleisch.
Whatever transpired, Johann
would always know that he had
Peter and Johannes to come back to.

AFTER AN INTER-CLASS STRUGGLE, THE GENSFLEISCH AND
SOME OTHER PATRICIAN FAMILIES ARE BANISHED FROM THE
CITY. JOHANN LEAVES MAINZ WITH HIS BROTHER FREILE
AND WITH HIS BRONZE DOG, FUGUE. THEY ARE GOING TO
STRASBOURG.

Disconnecting the Colors

The sky, its flow and flight,
the different grays—
their codes not known.
Departing in a particular
February, the knobs of
the trees cold, and all of the roofs dark.

Back of them, over Germany receding,
the packed-in hills:
the secure limits, looking back.

We are always in some measure
changing colors; moving from band
to band on the ranking seas.

Jogged in a cart, with their
luggage: the horses' imprints
left alphas and omegas on the
road; the iron itself went
on—the shoes kept going.

Johann carried the tools
of a goldsmith in his satchel.
In his stomach, a dread of
desertion from the family:
but the family fortunes were
over, he thought, in Mainz.

Bent like an autumn leaf against
the weather, his brother, Freile
was angry to leave his comforts
and the voices at home that
called him: "Freile, the farrier."
Like Johann, not wholly dependent on
rents and annuities, he liked
his trade.
                    They came
to the place of embarkment.
"Do not look back."
The horses were sidling and stepping
the lavish banks—the brothers wrapped
in furs like wealthy patrons;
and a small, flat boat awaiting
belonging to peasants.

They rode on the ancient Rhine,
and thought of Gutenberg: the estate
of their mother, Else . . .
. . . not to see her again.

Then outside Strasbourg,
more water than Johann imagined,
even in tales: the Ile and the Rhine
both rocking, toppling his
territory: Johann holding fast
to his tools in the fields of motion.

Moving from gray to pigments
of rocks and weeds, he led
the way, his distant stomach
hurting with various hungers:
the wooden ship
rising and falling—a leaf
on the tide—the brothers
moved forward and away from
the balancing waters.

GUTENBERG IN STRASBOURG

Courtships & Courtrooms/
The Beginnings of Print

IN STRASBOURG, GUTENBERG WAS UNABLE TO BUY
MATERIALS FOR HIS CRAFT. IN THE CITY SQUARE, ACROSS
FROM THE TOPPLING CATHEDRAL, HE SETS UP A SHOP TO
SELL MIRRORS AND POLISHED STONES.

If He Thought of Mainz

If he thought of Mainz,
he thought of it old,
an iron stove of a city—
with sober buildings and cobbles
that led to familiars.
                    In Mainz
it was always Family Uber Alles,
and business safely contained
in the sinews of families.
He was Henny Gensfleisch, third
child of Freile and Else.
He had worked in the City Mint
beside his relatives, had enjoyed
a loving woman for a night,
a brace of falcons, an arduous
life in the trades.
                He would miss
haphazard feasts, the steins of beer,
the bones under foot, the laps, the dogs,
clamor of uncles. By raging fires,
the righteousness of the Gensfleisch.

             Arriving a new place,
Strasbourg, everything shining—
at any turn the buildings took him
further, beams and projectiles
rose up in diamonds and pentacles.
His heart beat fast and he found
himself feeling his future. Here
the chimney-pots were of rosy brick,

the languages various. The skies
were blowing with flapping clouds
in percussive March, the guilds
all flying their flags.

Ann saw him first; she was
visiting the market—
among the fruit stalls, holding
a sober melon—weighing its merits.

Tall, before his shop, fine as a flag,
Johann was turning a key in a lock
as one who made it. A man with
secrets in his cloak, she thought,
an Alchemist; perhaps a trader
in old brass, an interpreter
of signs.

He saw her also, who had decided
leaving Mainz, to avoid alliances.

Her arm was strong, the sun revolved
on her expert pivots: a device
of threads on her bosom, swing
of the skirts: she was all in black
but not mournful, her face a cosmos.
Her movements were sure, using
sunlight, not wasting a minute.

Two walked beside her, to help
with her horse and the melons.
To be one of these was all Johann's wish—
he was careful to think instead
"I will not be your carrier."

But Gutenberg settled,
a goldsmith without a guild,
to pay his taxes in Strasbourg.

DUE TO ITS FAVORABLE LOCATION AT THE CROSSROADS OF
CARAVAN ROUTES AND WATERWAYS, STRASBOURG WAS AN
IMPORTANT SETTLEMENT SINCE THE BRONZE AGE. IT
ACHIEVED PROMINENCE DURING THE REIGN OF
CHARLEMAGNE, AND BY 1200 WAS FOSTERING THE RISE OF
AN ENTERPRISING MIDDLE CLASS. IN THE FIFTEENTH
CENTURY IT BECAME A FREE REPUBLIC GOVERNED BY A
COUNCIL MADE UP OF REPRESENTATIVES OF THE GUILDS.

What Was North to the Talkative Franks

What was North to the talkative Franks
was the South to Johann,
full of light and heat.

Freile said the people
had heads as alike as cabbages;
that their whiskers were
clipped like dogs' . . .

But Johann was thinking of
how at home he was in a place
more beautiful than Mainz where
the lanes were dark,
the Elders reticent.
Now these wide streets . . .

They were watching the people
scattered like thrown grain—
splendidly bright and singular
in mid-morning, right under
the steep cathedral.
In the open plaza,
the leaves on the bushes
were stiff, unyielding and
rattling like pieces of silver.

The people were doing business
pointing forefinger or arm.

Johann thought of himself
as a part of an upper class,
and enforced his patrician status
on entering Strasbourg;
but he envied the crafty
insolence of tradesmen.

Freile was missing the family
greedily in a place where
nobody called him by his name,
as "Freile, the farrier."
And Fugue, the dog, gave him
asthma.
            Hard on benches
the brothers sat, crowding
the locals at elbow with
their Northern furs, and wearing
heavier metal medallions.

Johann urged Freile to stay
with him in Strasbourg, as they
listened to Southern speech.
Freile replied that in Strasbourg
they spoke with a mumbling
of lap-dogs.

Outside in the square people
crowded into chocolate houses
or talked together and
leaned on reliable statues.

Safe in a tavern, with
his Gensfleisch brother
drinking and growling, Johann
did not suspect that later,
in an even more foreign city,
a statue would stand unmoved
in any weather: while bus-drivers
shouted "Plaza Gutenberg"
and the figure in bronze looked
out over meadows of faces.

Mainz, Naples, and several other cities are represented by the same woodcut in the Nuremberg Chronicle.

ST. ARBOGAST WAS A FRANCISCAN CONVENT HOUSED IN A
LARGE AND ANCIENT ROMAN VILLA NEAR A SMALL ISLAND
IN THE RIVER ILE WHICH WAS DESTINED TO BE KNOWN AS
THE PRINTERS' ISLAND. THE SISTERS FOUND IT NECESSARY
TO RENT PART OF THEIR PROPERTY TO ENHANCE THEIR
SMALL INCOME. THEY WERE PART OF THE LOCAL PARISH
AND RAN A SCHOOL OF INSTRUCTION IN RELIGIOUS
OBSERVANCES AND LATIN GRAMMAR.

St. Arbogast

The Sisters of Mary[10] (who roll out
no lavish carpet) rented Johann
the Deacon's quarters. The Deacon
had died, and it was proper to rent
this property to a layman.
But they did penance daily
for letting him do his pounding
so close to the bones of Saints.

On his part Johann
gave hallelujahs of thanks
to do his work—through clouds
of metallic dust—
so close to the relics
enshrined by the hooded nuns.
"But perhaps," he thought,
"their hearing is very poor."
His work was noisy and grateful
to his needs. He liked
the secluded island, and Green Mountain
where he could get stones to polish.

---

10. Sisters of Mary, an invented Order.

Outside bird-chatter was bright
as a rattle of spoons. Unseen,
a sky-absorbing meteor passes
Orion. A new wind sits
on his shoulder.

It was polishing stones that
first brought Andrew, one of
the Drizehen family, Czechs
from Pilsen. They had
lived for years in Strasbourg,
but still were strangers.

In the Bible it says
a miracle gives a signal
in advance, when something
irreversible commences:
water covers rock in a thirsty
desert; the sun lights up a thorn.

Like an enthrallment, Andrew
slipped into Johann's life.
He was first in the city to find
Johann—except for Ann.
Andrew said nothing about
the Secret Art, though
rumors were floating like fog
above the city.

But Andrew only said that he came
by water. A small dry raft
had settled among the reeds,
the island green in the mirroring
water. The River Ile
is generous at low tide to sly
and willowy raftsmen.

In a while they were drinking
wine together—Johann, usually
taciturn—began to tell
something about his plans
for an Art that would
change the world. Andrew
believed at once in
the Secret Art, though Johann
at first taught him only
to polish stones.
    But soon, without
much thought, Andrew was
a partner. Together they
tried out moulds and inky
compounds: sizes of platens,
absorbency of linen,
suppleness of animal skins,
thickness of cloth.
                And when
it was no longer Autumn
and storms began, and the coal
was scarce and shining, and many
a draft-horse gone to the war
with the Armagnacs,[11] the coal-
sellers' stallion sold
to the bitter mercenary, Johann
and Andrew kept on working,
the light falling cold through
the broken and cat-sized window,

---

11. Armagnacs—Mercenaries attacking Alsatian cities in the service of
    the Duke of Gascony. It was the Armagnacs also, in a later war,
    who started the fires that burned most of the Gutenberg/Strasbourg
    records.

the Roman cement making cracks
in the ancient Convent.

Till they crowded a throng of words
on some scraps of paper:
and the passion for print
was on them like a Saviour.

THE DEATH OF JOHANN'S MOTHER WAS A LOSS THAT
BROUGHT OTHER LOSSES. SHE ALWAYS SUPPORTED THE
GENIUS OF HER FAVORITE SON, AND WHEN HE LEFT MAINZ,
JOHANN TURNED OVER TO HER TWO OF HIS ANNUITIES
FROM THE CITY. BUT HIS BROTHERS NEEDED THESE FUNDS
TO SHORE UP LOSSES, PETITIONED FOR THEIR TRANSFER
AND RECEIVED IT. NOR DID THE ESTATE OF ELSE BRING
THE WEALTH THE GENSFLEISCH EXPECTED.

Mirrors

Johann had other income due
from Mainz, but received
no payments honoring his credits.
Accustomed to money, he never
considered borrowing. When Andrew
offered a Drizehen loan, Johann
refused it. He only *thought*
about it, at the time.

With a passion, he needed
an object he could sell.
In one flash he thought of
the Alchemists—their paradoxical
search for Self—but abandoned that
and became enamored of mirrors.

They were old as Karnak, as old
as the papyrus that he wanted—
and he liked their blue light
when he pounded out steel
to his bumpy likeness: metal,
his element.

Now he saw a face that was
bold, set to a purpose,
eyes of Germanic question,

and sharply blue. The useful
hands; but still, an emigré,
alone as an actor: his future
as thin as a star.

In Nuremberg craftsmen made
mirrors out of glass;
Gutenberg used an alloy
from the hills near Colmar,
burnished to give a glow
to the viewer's face.

Many separations take place
in parting the self from the image:
the one residing in the little
glass, often more small than loveable—
the one in the full-length mirror
that we hope for: the soul's
equivalent, the strict companion.

Now dowagers came to buy.
Alive in his shop, their faces
entered his metals. Athwart
a profounder thought, or
over a shoulder, he'd look up
and say—"Frau-so-and-so?
Can I find you a treasure?—
this bracelet adorned with agate?"

("But leave O leave my mirror
when you go, and let me be
a pond without an image:
. . . without your fond pout,
without your brave feather,
without your smile.")

IN THE MID-FIFTEENTH CENTURY THE MOST POPULAR
VEHICLE FOR TRAVEL WAS STILL THE PILGRIMAGE, THOUGH
NOT AS RELIGIOUSLY INSPIRED AS IN SOME EARLIER
PERIODS. EVERY SEVEN YEARS A PILGRIMAGE GATHERED IN
AACHEN TO HONOR CHARLEMAGNE, WHOM GUTENBERG
HOPED MIGHT BE HIS ANCESTOR.

The Aachen Fair

Thanne longen folk to goon on pilgrimages[12]

Within a month Gutenberg
had a market for mirrors.
The news came pounding up
from the city streets,
bumping along with the cartsful
of beets and turnips—to market—
everything washed, and honored
for table or pot. The confident
vendors were holding vegetables
high by their succulent tops,
and shouting of bargains and pilgrims.

A pilgrimage would gather
this year in Aachen, in Charlemagne's
city, where his statue in pure gold
would bless the pilgrims.
Pilgrims want mirrors to wear,
ensconced at girdle. Johann
and Andrew made many—
the mirrors when finished
were everywhere, in closet,
on tables and chairs,
in wooden boxes.

---

12. Chaucer, Introduction to *The Canterbury Tales.*

For the pilgrim, the mirror
could absorb the image
of some saint, or a place
of miracle. It would stay always—
hidden inside the glass,
to meditate on and
match memory with.

        As it turned out,
the Church objected to selling
and buying, in the presence of
and at the time of, a Holy
Pilgrimage. Gutenberg lost
to ill-fortune his whole
investment. The only things
sold at Aachen were the Indulgences.[13]

---

13. Actually, the Fair was postponed until the following year.

Gensfleisch zum Gutenberg Coat of Arms

THE COAT OF ARMS OF THE GENSFLEISCH FAMILY SHOWS A HUNCHBACKED DWARF HOLDING A BEGGING BOWL. THE IMAGE IS ON A SHIELD LOCATED UNDER AN OVERRIDING, PROTECTIVE FIGURE. CHARLEMAGNE'S FATHER WAS KNOWN AS PEPIN THE SHORT, AND ONE OF HIS SONS—NAMED PEPIN—MIGHT HAVE BEEN A HUNCHBACK. GUTENBERG FELT THAT BECAUSE OF THIS SIMILARITY AND THE EMPEROR'S VENERATION OF LANGUAGE, CHARLEMAGNE MIGHT WELL HAVE BEEN HIS PATRON.

Charlemagne

Educated, but not to read or write—
to whistle up hawks, lead charges,
conquer at Tours; by force to convert
the German with the Paynim—War was
his mortal toil, and the sloth of Kings,
lingering in his thermal baths at Aachen.

. . . And the sloth of Kings—but this did not
corrode him, stretching out a lumbering frame
seven times his foot in length, as Alcuin said.[14]
He learned (not languished), Latin and Greek,
astrology and numbers; he could discuss
The Mabinogian[15] with scholars.

He sent to England for Alcuin, Sweden
for Einar, to start a knightly school—
but all was centered in the healing pool.

---

14. One of a number of personal descriptions Alcuin included in his *Life of Charlemagne*. The script he invented for Charlemagne is Miniscule.

15. *The Mabinogian*, a collection of Welsh tales.

Knighted, they thought him sworn to his seamless
self: splendid in war, but not at war within.
His edicts were not first written down;
he said them. Afterwards Alcuin would put
them in fair language.

His scribes devised a script
as small as rain and clear
as that, for use throughout
his empire. Charlemagne,
wearied by unkempt, fanciful
calligraphy, turned away:
he could never learn to write
his name, but he could govern.

He won over, rewarded, chastened
or eliminated most of the prominent
people of his day: survived.
. . . Survived so well that no one
could succeed him. At the last,
he dragged one foot.

On country roads,
by water, listening,
some thought he would be
coming back in Spring.

The Emperor Justinian

Manuel II

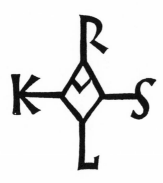

Charlemagne

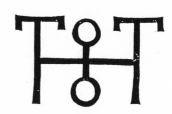

Otho the Great

The Signatures of Some Kings

WORRIED ABOUT THE LOSS OF HIS INVESTMENT, HIS
EXPERIMENTS WITH PRINTING NOT EVEN CLOSE TO SUCCESS
OR CLOSURE, GUTENBERG WALKS BESIDE THE RIVER ILE,
AND THINKS FOR THE FIRST TIME OF TRANSMITTING THE
HOLY BIBLE INTO MECHANICAL TYPE. HE FEELS BRIEFLY THE
WORLD-WIDE REPERCUSSIONS, HIMSELF AS AGENT. SHAKEN,
HE SEEKS OUT ANN OF THE IRON GATE.

There is an issue breaking
ahead of our knowledge . . .
As the bird breaks the hard sky,
a Word comes out of the ignorant air
surprising even the lark.
The receiver sees the Fatherland
die around him . . . his cranium
opens, he looks up, is alone.
The resurrection is in
his astonished face.

A Pastor shelters himself
in a throbbing cathedral;
he echoes Interpretations
of the times, helps people
to die, or rest, or look at
miniatures.

But what avatar does he
need, that first receiver—
be it Adam or Luther or
abstracted Gutenberg, seeing
through fog the wiry, German
illegible shapes of trees?
He has encountered force
out of air, a planet
visible to the naked eye
and gold as a grape.
He is foreign now; the bells

ring double, and chime
in an outer direction.

Stands there feeling
penniless as an arrow,
rich as an Angel.
The life-twist in him a knife,
he seeks out the woman
seeped in the ripening colors,
he saw in the market,
remembers the looks between
them that saturate. Goes to
Ann of the Iron Gate. . . .
She resounds like an anvil,
reckons with locks, undoes
her fortress, lets in
the man she remembers.

Under her manifold quilts
their passions connect through
a trembling bravado of knees.
Morning lets down out of sky
an ordinary day: their garish breakfast
of great potatoes and sweating sausages
returns them to status of householders:
she in her stronghold, he later returning
to his household in St. Arbogast where his
loved wines deepen in cellar, where he
will gather his printers.

Like loved animals, they help relieve
the ecstasy and boredom of his
Secret Art. And his absolute
attention to that changed everything:
all Holy Days, all saints, all calendars,
all illiterate men, all
other predictable unions.

JOHANN BECOMES MORE AND MORE WORRIED THAT SOME
OTHER INVENTOR MAY BRING MECHANICAL TYPE TO
COMPLETION. HE HIMSELF HAS FONTS OF ALPHABETS,
PASSABLE INK AND PARCHMENT. AS FAR AS HE KNOWS NO
ONE ELSE HAS THOUGHT ABOUT MOVEABLE TYPE. HE HAS
THE LETTERS AND PAPER, BUT NO CONVENIENT WAY TO
IMPRESS THE ONE WITH THE OTHER. THE SECRET ART IS
GIVEN FURTHER IMPETUS IN OBSERVING A WINE PRESS.

Ann and Johann: A Day in the Wine Country

They walked in a scorch of light
in the talented fields—the egrets
long and lengthening, embarrassed
by love; their thin, homely
faces averting—nodding,
shaking off minutes.

The sun in that wine-making country
was strong and white. Johann
felt it in flushes, igniting
his other dream.
              Ann's hand
was sweet as the touch
of a distant seal—playful,
far off. Then close and cold,
then warm.
            Rings of golden
sun encircled his fingers.
He felt touch multiply,
enhanced by the elegant metal—
the flowers saying nothing
in simple crowds.

Then vaulting and mysterious
the winery: wooden as memory,
overlapping with shadows.

The vaults held only wine:
not men, not sounds.
Held barrels. Held drums.

Closer, the wine-press,
its slow half-turning motion
starting the vintage—
the ages mattering,
the value preserved.

CROP CHANGES WERE NOT UNUSUAL TO REJUVENATE
ARABLE LANDS. FORMERLY A BREWERY, THE WINERY NOW
PROCESSED GRAPES FROM A NEW VINEYARD. IT WAS THE
CUSTOM FOR PROPRIETORS TO OFFER WINE TO VISITORS. A
WINE CONNOISSEUR, GUTENBERG ORDERED SOME CASES
TO BE SENT TO ST. ARBOGAST, ONE FOR THE SISTERS OF
MARY WHO, FROM TIME TO TIME, WERE EXPECTED TO
ENTERTAIN THE MONSEIGNEUR FROM THE CATHEDRAL.

The Winery: Ann

She was sensuous. She loved
the taste of a lip, the success
of passion, and words to enhance
or diminish: and always those
times of accident or boredom,
when amour ran its course
and then burst into flowers
of fire.
        With her late husband—
(But imagining other lovers)—
no times so enjoyable as these
with Johann. There are times
when the partner's feet become
immortal—standing and waiting
while she digresses—
waving an ample corset.

Or walking single-hearted
a field of summer. In Alsatian
sun the hills are shaggy as sheep
in back of the gold-tinged vineyards—
the sun on her arms that hold
the hamper of cheeses, the bread
of the splendid grains. A summer
not like any other, and lasting

as long as it stayed—she happy
to serve it. And now it came
again, filling her arms and
breathing like warm grass.

The Winery: Johann

And Ann beside him—now
not strange, but calm and close—
as out of the blazing day
his dog came lumbering,
lay down in a shadow near them—
breathing and stretching.

In confidence Johann returns
with her through the fields,
clouds inhabiting the sky—
April, rolling and mapping
the country.

Why should they separate?—
he to St. Arbogast and she
to the stony house behind
the iron gate?

(They went to Ann's.)

He remembered one day as he was
leaving Mainz, alone on an ancient
road the Romans built, he had
taken his sandals off to feel
the turf. "Not to leave home,"
he thought. "Not to leave earth."

The Printing Press

Gutenberg saw that he couldn't
design it himself. He called on
Conrad Saspach, the wood-turner.
Much splintering of wood, and Conrad
made him a spine for the press—
a spiral cylinder more beautiful,
Johann thought, than the Venus
of Melos. It could raise or lower
a platen to press out words.
Envisioned first, then built.

Johann, now bursting to teach
his Secret Art,[16] called Hans Riffe and
Anthony, brother of Father Heilmann.
They paid him substantial sums,
he swore them to secrecy.
Other apprentice printers came
to St. Arbogast; a fellowship began—
the wife of Lorenz Beildeck cooked
the dinners, put extra places at
table, glasses for wine.

For a while they copied some
pages from a Donatus—a Latin
grammar then in general use—
on handmade paper, or odd shaped
scraps of parchment.

---

16. In the records of the many lawsuits in which Gutenberg was
    involved, his invention was always referred to as "his Secret Art,"
    never as "printing."

            The valuable
scraps went through hands of various
sizes seeming soft, or brittle,
but looking like other scraps.
Most were scattered or burned.

Later Johann began to fear
that other craftsmen would learn
about the structure of his press;
four interlocking parts that
held it solid: the wooden spiral
that gave it vertical motion;
the freedom of moveable type.

IN THE FIFTEENTH CENTURY, THERE WERE NO COPYRIGHT LAWS. INVENTORS KEPT THEIR SECRETS WELL GUARDED, AND CHEFS THEIR RECIPES. FEARING THE PRESS WOULD BE SEEN AND COPIED, GUTENBERG MOVED THE NEW INVENTION TO THE HOME OF ANDREW DRIZEHEN.

The Cleaning Woman

The Cleaning Woman made short
shrift of the press when it
came to cleaning Andrew
Drizehen's bedroom. This polyglot
house was bad enough anyway:
you could hear Czech words
or Frankish, every day.
What she did, was take her time,
and tend to Andrew. It was cold
enough in Strasbourg; coal was
scarce; and the contraption
looking sad there
as an ostrich. Part wood,
part ancestor, with a leaning
slant . . . cold, needing
a shirt . . . she had no time
to feel sorry for anything new.
Andrew was strange enough.

Andrew dreamed the press
was like himself—a new
transfiguration. He used all
the family inheritance to help
keep it in paper, in ink, in
secrecy and in order. And he called
the contraption Hans.

Andrew told her devices like
the press would some day do
the work, and men could rest.
As God created earth, and let
men run it; men could create
devices that could learn.
A press, he said, could learn
to be a press.
                    But the Cleaning
Woman cared only about Andrew.
She tried to keep him from
drafts and complications.
The worst was when his partner
came in at night, and Andrew
would hop from his bed, thin
as a mantis, and help him—
getting ink spots on the sheets,
banging one chunk of wood
against another. The family
closed themselves
behind their doors.
Andrew had told them
soon they would be rich.
And when that happened,
the Cleaning Woman told him,
she would ask for a golden
guilder and feather duster.

Finding Itself Invented

All future words are mine
to liberate or conserve:
no letter should be confined
to one strict page, nor struck
for all time in a diphthong.

Old letters, their legibility
impaired, should not be thrown
in open sewers or rivers,
but placed in a font with
a medley of similar others:
some smaller than ants, some
larger than blooming azaleas—
yet all shall be S's or A's
or significant Q's or P's.
                    Some printers
may follow the secular order:
from Alpha and Beta to Zed
kept safe in their families—
Gothic or Miniscule, or sensuous
Italic from Florence. My children—
work where ye list!
You are made of the sturdiest lead.

Soon words shall be honored in
lengthy and dignified order
for all to employ, not Dukes
nor Doctors merely; calligraphers
may now retire to Lake Como
or other sequestered environs,
with their fanciful spellings
and capitals made of lace.

Sturdy and practiced,
printed words are uniform,
their grammar is sure and proud,
and curbed by usage, by known
consent from Aristotle or Lucretius.

Dictionaries shall be honored
more than Bibles: illumination
replaced by actual illustrations.

Each word shall be made
From definitions tried and true,
created by stalwart letters—
O words—take place!

UNATTACHED WOMEN OFTEN WERE HIRED AS
HOUSEKEEPERS IN RETURN FOR BOARD AND ROOM.
THOSE WITH FAMILIES CULTIVATED COUSINS, TRAVELLING
TO SEVERAL THROUGHOUT THE YEAR AND HELPING WITH
CHILDREN OR NEEDLE WORK. KINGS AND QUEENS WITH
THEIR RETINUES DID THIS ALSO, "HOLDING COURT" IN
VARIOUS PARTS OF THEIR REALMS—AN HONOR DREADED
BY SOME OF THEIR DISTANT RELATIVES.

Andrew Drizehen's Funeral

When they had the funeral
the printing press was present
looking not unlike
the deceased partner:
Mechanical, off-hand,
accidentally
to-be-or-not-to-be
at the wholesome funeral.

Both of them were
presentiments.

Andrew Drizehen had died
without by-your-leave on Christmas.
His horrified sisters were
wringing their hands and crying,
trying to domesticate everything:
potholders and hot bricks
in the dim light, bedpans
and waterbags all courted
lest they get away like Andrew.
While the women made German pasties
shaped like angels,
Niklaus, Andrew's brother-in-law,
wound the clocks. Looked to see
what was kept in Andrew's
hamper and strong-box.

The women were saying,
"He died of the lateness of hours,"
"Of choking and wheezing,"
"Of an ear infection
brought on by poisonous ink."
"And all of our money
devoured by his alchemist partner."

Now all they had was
his lengthy wooden frame
on the mild bed.
"He can come to rest at last
in a beautiful coffin,
his parts composed."
"But who will dispose
of the monster?"

The partner got there
while they were looking at it:
the Press, its elbow jiggered
its jaw a-jab.

Gutenberg, furiously well-dressed
and nervous with gifts,
was a Gentleman let in
by a cousin from Pilsen.
She held an embroidery frame
on which she stitched
the life-dates of the deceased.
Some other relatives sat
on a parlor sofa: ready to serve,
but holding themselves
out of the limelight.

Johann took small mirrors
from velvet pockets; still stung
by the cancellation of the fair at Aachen
he was glad there was some small
use for his pilgrims' mirrors.

To the sisters he showed
his contract with their brother
on vellum, in German script.
The contract, he said, was ended
with Andrew's life. No heirs
were possible.[17] The women blinked.
Stunned by stolid blackness
of the print, they thought
they were trafficking with Beelzebub.

They didn't understand what
Johann said, but were excited,
and they wanted to keep
the mirrors.

Johann sent for Conrad Saspach, the wood-
turner who made the Press.
He took out four wooden pieces
from the Press, and it wouldn't
work without them. The family
hid them in a sewing cabinet.
The bars of type were placed
Under attic ledges.

---

17. Niklaus, the brother-in-law of Andrew, tried to break the contract,
but he lost the case in court. Gutenberg was instructed to pay the
Drizehen family 37 guilders, the amount owed them after
subtracting the cost of providing Andrew with food and drink for
quite a number of days.

On a shelf by the Press were
utensils of foreign origin,
droppings of lead,
the carpets sullied with oils.

Johann wanted the Press removed
to an entrance alcove where
people would pass by quickly.
They covered it under two
of Andrew's shirts, with
a tapestry on top.
Conrad and Johann
moved the furniture so fast
some thought they hadn't
touched it.

Gutenberg came to the funeral.
He stood close to the dark alcove,
nodding at mourners.

                They came
through the vestibule bursting
to comfort survivors: filling
the household with grief
as with a tide: the underwater
sounds, gestures of seals . . .
the words were bobbing like floats.

In the parlor the body shone
with a radiance of corpses.
And Gutenberg thought how
the marvelous wooden spiral
had turned like a sea,
and the Press had worked:
he thought Andrew was seeing it now
with his permanent gaze, in back of
his not altogether unseeing eyes . . .

IN 1435, A CITIZEN FROM MAINZ (OR OTHER GERMAN CITY)
WAS LIABLE FOR A DEBT INCURRED BY HIS HOME CITY TO
ANY CITIZEN IN THE CITY TO WHICH HE TRAVELLED. THE
CITY OF MAINZ WAS IN ARREARS IN PAYING A NUMBER OF
ANNUITIES TO JOHANN GUTENBERG, TO WHICH HE WAS
ENTITLED. BUT THE CURRENT REGIME IN MAINZ SHOWED
NO INCLINATION TO MAKE THE PAYMENTS. THE CITY
CLERK WAS ON HIS WAY TO STRASBOURG TO ATTEND
HIS DAUGHTER'S WEDDING.

The City Treasurer

The Clerk of the City treasured
the City's money. He treasured
his daughter also, but she was
in Strasbourg, becoming accustomed . . .

She stayed with the family
of her fiancé getting used to his
Mother's culinary arts, to their
quilting patterns and ways
of pillowing feathers.

            At weddings
fathers come to see their daughters
look beautiful; also to lose them.
Herman Krug was losing many guilders
to have the wedding. But these bought
sauerkraut and palpable krullers
and wine from fragrant barrels.
He expected that. What he didn't
expect was Gutenberg. Herman arrived
with a father-in-law brightness—
good clothes and clean-licked shoes.
He was stopped by a Deputy brought
by Lorenz Beildeck, Johann's tired
servant. "The Gensfleisch had

the Mainz Clerk thrown in gaol,"
people said. This raised
the status of Gutenberg
more than his invention would.

Johann went to the gaol to see
the prisoner. "If you are released,
you'll swear to pay the money.
At six percent . . ." which was usual
for that time. Herman explained
that he didn't have it with him. It was
something over eighty or ninety
guilders. They made arrangements.

About the arrest, Johann apologized.
He said his servant
had misunderstood.
Herman, in turn, invited him
to the wedding. Johann realized
he must bring Ann.
                    Lorenz Beildeck
drove them in Ann's substantial
carriage. He could come along
and eat in the family's kitchen
and boast about Johann Gutenberg
and the mysteries of invention.

Weddings in Strasbourg

In Strasbourg weddings were
always taking place—many in churches
like St. Thomas' with growing grape
vines lofting the terraces; in chapels
sponsored by nobles—some near
a fountain.
                        In the dark cathedral
with few witnesses, a confessor
and penitent whisper behind curtains:
an absolution waves the uncolored air.

Ann would like the weddings to
happen all at once; or to watch a wedding barge
on the River Ile rise and be set down
on the Island at Green Mountain—
near St. Arbogast. She had never seen
Johann's stronghold.
                        He was knocking
things over and looking for his boots.
He only thought of boots when he was
in them. She had told him days ago
his boots were dreadful, and sent for
Schotten Awel, gossip and cobbler,
because he sewed leather quickly.

Johann was furious. He hadn't heard
her say it. His mind was occupied
with something pressing. He was
wondering why he agreed
to go to this wedding. He had scarcely
the gold, any more, to make Ann
some earrings. All was fine
when they were alone, each singular—
the world not knowing.

unopened, curling at edges—even
Johannes Fust wanting from Johann
his share of their workshop's taxes.

And Peter Schoeffer in Mainz was
finding out that marriage for him
is the short way home: he had
married Fust's daughter.
                              Out of
a morning window Johann saw the gables,
a skyful of fog, and on the ground
a curfew of autumn leaves.
                              In the end,
he had to wear the boots
of Ann's late husband.
They were made of pigskin; she had
saved them and had them repaired
by Schotten Awel. Johann felt
like a misplaced sailor, a fraudulent
husbandman; a person assigned
to a woman.
                 But for Ann's sake
he went to the celebration
in her carriage. They got to
a wedding together—(thanks
to Lorenz Beildeck)—though
it wasn't theirs.

The Breach

I.

In a sharp morning, at six
or earlier bells . . . seemed to
gather around her, a curious
weather. Something came down—
not a dove—and rendered her
doubtful. She felt he was going
to leave her. Sudden as wind,
she went to St. Arbogast.

When she drove in the yard,
the cock crowed in a spiral.
Johann rose to the occasion—
went to meet her.
He kissed her strongly,
and felt his elements change:
he was made of yeast. And he
thought what love can do
to the serious stomach.
She said she believed his jewelry
stoutly made, with excellent
precision in his workshop—
but not in his house,
surrounded by vile practices.
As soon as she smelled the retorts
and furnaces, she knew there was
more to his work than pilgrim's mirrors.
There was much he hadn't told her.

And St. Arbogast! was this like a house
of Mainz that Johann came from?
Were these the men he fed? . . .
who drank his wines? . . . the one
who bent over cauldrons
boiling something that looked like

persimmons, those others
bending wires and latches; and the silent
servant, who hated her as an adder.

Lorenz Beildeck already was packing
pincers and tongs, and good Alsatian
cloth for use in Mainz, and excellent
wines, while Johann scarcely realized
his life was stretching him in two
directions—the debts, the secret
formulae, the broken promises
all trailing him—especially one
to Ennelin, zu der Iserin Thure,
she of the Iron Gate.

The Breach

II.

Gutenberg's passion for his secret art
wouldn't hold a candle to Ann's rage.
She had thought him a haughty figure
in his shop, where the captains came
in their gear, more alert than clocks—
but now—a stranger, an oddity,
brother of Alchemists.

Match by match by match and candle
by candle, she started fires:
crackles of attention drew everyone
to them. Ann went public.
Encompassing as a parable
she was everywhere,
slamming her skirts to her ankles.
She was Ennelin zu der Iserin Thure,
not to be left but by death—
and one had achieved that already—
Karl, her husband, breeder of horses—
Now this fine handsome.

In anger now by daylight
she carries her own packages—
her lentils, her pounds of lard:
not letting her servants help her,
guards her colanders. She scrubs
her cats. She is bright
as soap at morning. She is salt.

By night she sleeps twice hard
among rattling carriages,
cinching her hair in the cap
of the velvet tassels.

In dark she disappears—
none of your half-light.
She is purchaser of her goods:
she has no debts.

In the town square Johann
feels himself looked at:
scrutiny fixes him,
mixed with a yapping of dogs.
He who had been sure of a past
and of a future, son of a Family,
goldsmith, master of servants.
"He is a charlatan," say
the burgomasters; "none but
a shaman would gamble a solid
life on a visionary future.
He is likewise in arrears in his taxes."

The Marketplace

What we say is clouded,
but what we do not say
is clear to everyone—it is
what they come for:
the dandies at hangings;
the listeners-for-love at a sermon;
in the bulging market,
those plumed for a bibulous time.

Raised on a dais at Strasbourg,
imagine a speaker—his mouth
emitting the colors of fashion
or crime—while anyone knows
the wishes, the smells,
the wanderlust—the oranges
he wanted, his wounds that
are treasured liked diamonds.

Now coming away from the church
with a piece of the relic,
the high-riding clergy appear,
as foolish as ostriches . . .
Who does not guess the motives
unknown to the riders?

Unused to publicity, which his
art would soon make common,
Gutenberg claimed immunity—
he believed in established
privacy for the gentry.

Away from the public market,
trying out letters, he had forged
his alphabets—some thick and
German, some tiny as bird-claws.
At night he imagined them live
on the dead-white page . . .

*   *   *

In a distant Century
a boy breaks the morning's green glass
throwing The Journal across
my ordinary doorstep.
Gutenberg's letters and fonts—
by now outmoded—reach us
through younger carriers . . .
And the news keeps coming . . .

GUTENBERG, WORN OUT WITH CONTRACTS THAT
CRACKLED WHEN HE UNROLLED THEM AND REMINDERS
OF INTEREST DUE, FACED A DIFFERENT KIND OF SUIT.
FRIENDLY CREDITORS—LIKE ST. THOMAS' CHURCH IN
STRASBOURG— WERE BECOMING RESTIVE. HE WROTE TO
HIS BROTHERS IN MAINZ TO HELP HIM SAVE THE FAMILY
HONOR. THEY WOULD BE PROUD OF HIM, BUT NOT YET.
HE ALSO OWED MUNICIPAL TAXES AND A CONSIDERABLE
WINE-TAX, IN STRASBOURG.

The Summons

The trouble, when it came,
was in the air, the day was
wrapped in concealing fog—
unearthly. Even Green Mountain
looked virulent rather than
verdant. Burying a bone,
the dog tore up the garden.

For the first time, the River Ile
seemed polluted, with garbage
floating sideways and slowly
turning.
        A notice was handed
Johann by the baker who came
on alternate days to bring
the bread. Some hireling from
the Court who had not wanted
to cross the river to Arbogast
so early, had given the baker
a sack of meal to bring it.

Ann was suing Johann for
Breach of Promise—the news
already was spread abroad
by Schotten Awel, everyone

who stared at it transfixed.

The script of the document
was done in the popular "Bastard."
Johann knew that he could read,
but could she write? He had
never asked her. It was written
perhaps by the scribe near
the cobbler's stall—in the market
where he first saw her.
He tore it in two, then folded
the pieces into his wallet.

Johann preferred that disasters
came unannounced: storm, if it's
going to rain: no squeezing out
drops. Cloudburst was better
than sneaking from shower to
shower. But the day was dry.
He couldn't imagine rain.

Hauled into court like a common
criminal! This time was different—
he couldn't send Lorenz Beildeck.

He went to see the Brothers
of St. Thomas. The Brothers
could talk abstractly, like
the Alchemists. That day, it made
his head feel full of granite.

But they made the best absinthe[18]
in the city of Strasbourg.
Leaving, he wished for a storm

---

18. Absinthe or cassis or pernod.

Leaving late, he wished for a storm
to abolish logic. Instead
the tall stars were already
stretching from point to point.

Johann went back to Arbogast
to hope for sleep, and think
of the incontrovertible
loss of Ann.

UNLIKE THE ECCLESIASTICAL LEGAL SYSTEM IN MAINZ, THE
COURT AT STRASBOURG WAS UNDER THE JURISDICTION OF
THE HOLY ROMAN EMPEROR WHOSE IMPERIAL COURT WAS
SITUATED AT ROTTWEIL. BECAUSE OF THE DISTANCE, A
PROCURATOR WAS EMPOWERED TO JUDGE LOCAL CASES.
THESE PROCEEDED WITH CONSIDERABLE INFORMALITY.
ALL CITIZENS COULD ATTEND; MANY WANTED TO BE
WITNESSES.

The Courtroom

Gathered in the courtroom,
the tattling and shrewd—
inglorious: nobody willing to let
reason strike like a match
in the heat of the morning.

Outside the sun was moving
the grateful clocks: sun dials
and brilliant contraptions
of the times; while indoors
carrying out the laws,
Eternity fretted and bulged.

Ann was all in black, again
reminding those who addressed
her, she still was a widow
of substance. Wheels of attention
surrounding, she looked toward
the entrance, waiting, and even
for this—Johann was not punctual.
He would lose the case to her
if he did not come.

Later her servants would
not speak to his.

The courtroom in those days
was a chance to shine. People
scrubbed and sewed up in their
seams were sitting far forward,
opinions flying like pennants.
The Justice, very old, came
well-attended by henchmen carrying
maces close to their ears. All rose
in a silence of shuffling feet.

The Justice, already sweating
in ritual black, his prescribed
spoonful of pre-dawn brandy gone—
and his early breakfast—was
thinking of noon collation.
Just as the Bailiff was summoning
all to quiet, some sailors came in
and threw down their ropey gear.
They brought, as loud as a bell,
the salt of the sea.
They asked how the Love Match
went, and were rebuffed—though
others were talking and betting
in ardent whispers.
             As the Bailiff
was showing the sailors out: Arriving,
the Herr Defendant, before fastening
of the gates. His character witnesses
followed: Lorenz Beildeck; his wife;
Conrad Saspach, wood-turner, who made
the Press; goldsmith Hans Dunne;
and Andrew Heilmann with Father
Anthony Heilmann, Andrew's brother—
who well knew priests who served
the Imperial Court at Rottweil.

The many rings of the Justice
shown well in a nervous interim,
the connecting fingers
tapping the wooden table.

Upstairs in a loft
and belonging to no Order,
a statue of St. Michael
(now somewhat outmoded)
Defender of Justice
who passes no judgment
but Heaven's—is waited upon,
is holding the Balancing Scales.

IT WAS THE MOST LITIGIOUS OF TIMES. PEOPLE HAD JUST DISCOVERED THAT THEY COULD SUE EACH OTHER AND WERE TESTING THEIR LEGAL LIMITS IN THE COURTS. WITHIN THREE OF FOUR YEARS, GUTENBERG HAD AT LEAST A DOZEN SUITS AGAINST HIM, BY PEOPLE WHO WANTED TO SHARE IN HIS INVENTION, OR TO WHOM HE HAD INCURRED DEBTS. ONE SUIT WAS FOR LIBEL: ANOTHER FOR BREACH OF PROMISE.

Schotten Awel — Character Witness Against the Defendant

Schotten Awel took over
the Breach of Promise hearing
by speaking his mind and giving
imagination full vent. He loved
to be called up by the Court,
and often was: he had a reputation
of knowing more about everyone
in Strasbourg than the peeping Toms
themselves, and he was proud.
On occasion he cried out, and
stamped his well-shod feet,
being a cobbler. He was in
the habit of remaking shoes
for friends and familiars;
he would like to have kept
the boots of the Herr Professor—
when the so-called Gentleman
failed to come after them.

He came in a fortnight.

Schotten Awel said the Herr
Professor, Doctor, or Gentleman
as you cared to call him, had
terrible tempers. These were

to be avoided. He had thrust
his fist (when he finally
came to the cobbler's) through
a hard-sewn seam in the boots
to show they were useless.
The courtroom was quiet,
to hear more.
                    Then Schotten
Awel began to mention something
about a brothel, but
Father Heilmann rose and stopped
him. Some others said Schotten
Awel always said that. By now
a number of people were standing.
The Justice was pounding
his gavel and overwhelmed.

Gutenberg rose, and dominated.
He called the cobbler "A miserable
wretch who made his living
by lying and stealing."
                    Schotten
replied that he was suing Johann
for defamation of character.
After a wealth of shouting
the ancient Justice finally
prevailed. The Breach of
Promise suit was superceded,
and it was decided, almost
by those in the courtroom,
that Gutenberg should give
the cobbler fifteen guilders:
if he won in the larger suit
and proved his good character,
then Schotten would be
obliged to give them back.

If Gutenberg lost, he lost
in both court actions.

Gutenberg won in both;
the Justice finally got
his meal. No one in Strasbourg
ever forgot Schotten Awel.

THE RETURN TO MAINZ

The Foreclosure/The Bible

The Return to Mainz

Ann had sued him for Breach of Promise—
that was part of it; the Drizehens
decided the Printing Press should be
theirs; and the Parish at St. Thomas'
demanded payment for outstanding debts.
The disreputable cobbler testified
in court to the terrible temper
of the great "Herr Doctor."

Ann's case was thrown out of court
and that of the Drizehens—
but Gutenberg had to give
15 Kronen to the insulted cobbler.

Now in the town square Johann
felt himself looked at: scrutiny
fixing him, mixed with a yelping
of dogs.
      He thought of a time,
at the mint, when making money
was simply making money.

He remembered one day as he was
leaving Mainz, alone on a battered
road built by the Romans;
he had shaken his boots out briefly
to feel home turf.

           The exile
had long been over. Now
the longing for the ancient family
bond was rising in him again
like the sound of rain.

Portrait of Gutenberg

CARRYING HIS MOVEABLE FONTS OF LETTERS, TO MOVE
BACK INTO THE FIRM OF FUST AND GUTENBERG, JOHANN
LEAVES STRASBOURG. HE KNOWS THAT THE PRODUCTION
OF THE BIBLE WITH MOVEABLE TYPE WILL BE THE MAJOR
ACHIEVEMENT OF HIS LIFE, AND CAN'T WAIT TO DEVOTE
HIMSELF TO THAT EXCLUSIVELY. THOUGH WITH BEILDECK
AND SPOUSE, JOHANN SENSES HE IS ALONE. FREILE LEFT
LONG AGO, STILL HATING STRASBOURG.

Schoeffer and Fust

Alone, on a larger boat
and looking backward, Johann
carried his moveable letters
and fonts.

Watching the waves trail,
memories unroll: the streak of light
on the beach, the sun's step-ladder,
the ultimate break in the weather.

And constancy ticking away
like a feathered bomb.

Gutenberg had a real if mortgaged
connection with his co-workers,
Fust and Schoeffer, fellow-engravers—
last left, and first encountered
at the turn. For what was to come,
for Gutenberg, they were to be
simply the latest move
in the moon's disorder.

He could see their faces flicker
down corridors, in candle light—
no match for the moon's veranda.

He had left three ghosts behind
when he came from Mainz—
looking down roads and waterways
after him. He would recognize
Johannes Fust and Peter Schoeffer
but not himself
in his role
of insolvent debtor.

But he was alive
and seven years past forty.
He was first and best
in his trade—and he was
not yet cast in bronze.

IN MAINZ JOHANN SETTLES DOWN AT GUTENBERG, HIS
MOTHER'S ESTATE, WITH HIS SISTER AND HER HUSBAND,
MARGARET AND KLAUS. THEIR MOTHER HAD DIED DURING
JOHANN'S RESIDENCE IN STRASBOURG. HE REESTABLISHES
CONTACT WITH HIS FRIEND AND PATRON, JOHANNES FUST,
WHO HAS CONTINUED IN BUSINESS WITH JOHANN'S
FORMER APPRENTICE, PETER SCHOEFFER, NOW FUST'S
SON-IN-LAW.

The Foreclosure

Each one was settling down into
who he was. In Strasbourg or Mainz—
it was clear that Johann Gensfleisch
would print a Bible that couldn't
be surpassed.
                    Younger than the others,
Peter would wait. He was trained
by the Master, and the Son-in-law
of patron Johannes Fust.

Johannes wanted his money back.
Not trained as a printer,
in the shop he was greeting customers—
sweeping up metal filings.
He couldn't break Gutenberg's habit
of stopping the presses (they had three
by now) and improving
the process every time he printed.
Now he was shaving minute filings
from each letter, placing letters
closer together, thus achieving
four extra lines to a page.
What a saving in costly vellum!

Fust preferred Peter's printing.
It looked just as good as Gutenberg's,
and Peter's goal was to get
the extravagant Bible finished.

Johann had borrowed from Fust
eight-hundred guilders, but the money
went faster, always, than the printing.
In a short time he needed guilders—
eight hundred more. Fust borrowed
to get it, but by now was furious.

Johannes Fust foreclosed
on the printing business; the firm
would henceforth be titled
"Shoeffer and Fust."

The hearing was held in an Augustinian
monastery—just outside city walls.
The rain was heavy, as if each
drop were weighted.
Some monks named Albertus and Everettdig
might have come forth,
most curious to look at
the evil inventor.
But Gutenberg never appeared.
He did not come to the hearing.

THE GUTENBERG BIBLE IS IN TWO VOLUMES, EACH
WEIGHING ABOUT TEN POUNDS.[19] IT IS LATIN AND PRINTED
IN THE HEAVY BLACK SCRIPT THEN STANDARD FOR
GERMANY. THE ILLUMINATION IS AS FINE AS IN ANY
HAND-COPIED VOLUME, THE MECHANICAL CALLIGRAPHY OF
HIGHEST QUALITY.

The Bible

In those days nobody
wanted to trash the Bible—
nor other books (until later,
Copernicus). There was prophecy
that men would later burn books
or rend them in intricate pieces—
but at the time they were trying
to get them, not get rid of them.

As soon as the Gutenberg issue
was out, printers everywhere were
making copies by the cart-load;
Johannes Fust was barely repaying
himself because the later volumes
(many without what was known to some
as vain decoration) were easily
purchased for less.
                  Johann Gensfleisch
was directing the work for Schoeffer
and Fust, as he always had.
When the Bible was done—
and it took years—he left them.
He took some tools of his trade
along with him; no one objected.

---

19.   Or so it seemed to this writer.

Other equipment was bought
by Dr. Hummery, a different
patron. What Gutenberg did
was to print, as he always had:
he kept on by keeping on . . .[20]
though he didn't write colophons,
nor sign his name.
                    You have to
leave the earth to see the earth,
and Johann Gensfleisch
had been to the moon and back.

What he held he would hold,
in the mirror of his mind,
and nothing rescind.

---

20. Gutenberg's most important work of this later period was known as
    "The Catholicon."

ARCHBISHOP BERTOLD OF HENNEBERG MAKES GUTENBERG
A COURTIER OF THE MAINZ ARCHBISHOPRIC, ASSURING HIM
A LIVING AND FORGIVING HIS DEBTS. REVERSING A FIRST
REACTION IN WHICH SOME CHURCHES "PROHIBITED"
PRINTED BOOKS, THE ARCHBISHOP HAS LONG HAILED THE
"MECHANICAL BIBLE" AS A GREAT ACHIEVEMENT.
GUTENBERG ENDS HIS DAYS AS A LAY BROTHER AT ST.
VICTOR'S MONASTERY IN MAINZ.

My Eyes Come Home

"My eyes come home, no longer
wanting to be type-founders:
in simple sacks they close,
resting their marbles.

"Arrogant eyes, what sights
have adorned your lenses!
I shut the lids, and what
do I see? A ceiling-full
of letters: Romans and
Miniscules, and sturdy
German Gothics. Sometimes
I see what printing cannot
reveal: tree-lights and fields;
impending, the change of a season.
At night, the muscular dark
that holds up the frittering
starlight.

"I put down heavy stove-lids
on fires within—(and in me
still!)—that melted
impetuous metals. O earthly
elements, how you did thrive
in the mines that were
my veins; I was your crucible.

"I remember each useful fault
where the iron buckled, or
a letter broke that was
perfect in my intent.

"I leave my life to those
deciding birds that carry
their slanting edges
over Strasbourg;

"While the wandering, lopsided
bird of my dreams that surrendered
the Word to me with exacting eyes
completes a life not mine:
what I become."

     *   *   *

The Brothers orbit their rounds,
awkward as rocks. No metal sharpens
their gaze, though the morning
comes. It is rolling as small
as mercury over the hills.

The Printing Press

IN 1574, THE ASTRONOMICAL MARVEL OF ITS DAY WAS
INSTALLED IN STRASBOURG'S ROSE-STONE CATHEDRAL TO
REPLACE A FOURTEENTH CENTURY CLOCK. ABOVE A
PERPETUAL CALENDAR ENCIRCLING THE GLOBAL UNIVERSE,
A FIGURE OF JESUS APPEARS TO EXPEL DEATH, PORTRAYED
AS A SKELETON STRIKING THE HOURS. AT TWELVE,
APOSTLES PASS IN A PROCESSION, AND ARE BLESSED BY
JESUS. THE CLOCK IS A TRIUMPH OF RENAISSANCE SKILLS
INVOLVING THE WORK OF A TEAM OF SCIENTISTS,
THEOLOGIANS, ARTISTS, ARCHITECTS, AND WATCHMAKERS.
THE TECHNOLOGY OF THE DAY IS CELEBRATED. FOR THREE
CENTURIES, THE STRASBOURG CATHEDRAL WAS THE
WORLD'S TALLEST BUILDING.

Transition, The Strasbourg Clock

The Strasbourg clock came
indoors from the sea, locketing the
tides of the ultramarine Kingdom:
Strasbourg, master of rivers.

Inside Church walls, no Saint
comprehending: now—this
minotaur, elaborate with symbols,
new dispenser of favors.

The shock becomes palpable as bells
rung by no clergy or old sexton
attack the nervous systems of many.
By rote, after centuries of silence,
obedient and disoriented,
the apostles walk by slowly
at noon and midnight,
animating the Cathedral.

Some believe less than before.

Defensive ladies say,
"My Father, the Clock-maker.
My father invented the great
time-turning wheel;
my mother invented the pillow."

The rafters shake as science
and theology get married.
Known after that
as The Cathedral,
not often as Notre Dame,
"Le Grand Ange Rose"
of Strasbourg[21] grew octagonal
to accommodate the change:
Jesus, our man of the hour, presides:
Godhead, moth of the evening,
touches her forehead with rose.

Now everywhere in the universe
tides glow and release
as seas surrender allegiance:
the planets encounter and pass
their appointed stars.
The moon is beneficent.

And concepts rage like bees.
Grace seems available.
The people learn. The clock
chimes away like a workman.

---

21. Paul Claudel.

THE REFORMATION BROUGHT "ARTIFICIAL WRITING"
INTO GREAT PROMINENCE. MARTIN LUTHER HAD A
BIBLE PRINTED IN GERMAN. NEW FORMS OF MEDIA
PROLIFERATED. AT THE BIBLIOTHÈQUE NATIONALE IN
PARIS YOU CAN SEE THE GUTENBERG BIBLE PASSING
BEFORE YOUR EYES ON MICROFILM. AT THE GUTENBERG
MUSEUM IN MAINZ, YOU CAN WATCH A FILMED VERSION
OF JOHANN'S LIFE.

The Puppet Show

When you go to the Mainz Museum
to see the Bible, you can also
see the life of Gutenberg. The actors,
marionettes, lend their forms to the story:
a story of debt and foreclosure by the patron.

They move with the grace and compassion
of Japanese dancers. Yet they are
German: wooden, casting no shadow,
heads tilted—resembling ovals
for darning stockings. They move
in a lemon light to act out the drama.

You would hardly think the former partners could
work together after that.
And yet, they did.
Directed by Gutenberg—these adversaries—these friends—
kept on until the Book was done.
It took seven years.
And the name of the firm
remained as Schoeffer and Fust.

By the time his book was finished
it wasn't his. But neither was it
anybody else's. The evidence remains—

though it carries no signature
nor colophon; and the concept
of a patent was unheard of.

In a gallery upstairs the Bible—
out of dark—is bright with
illumination: lettering of the Latin
boldly black; capitals of red
or gold—more decoration
than even a Monk could think of.

People said, surprised,
"You can hardly tell the difference."
And many who came
were not willing to pass on.

IN THE MIDDLE OF THE FIFTEENTH CENTURY, INTO THE
TALLEST CATHEDRAL IN EUROPE, AN ELABORATE ORGAN
WAS INSTALLED. PART OF ITS DECORATION INCLUDED
TWO WOODEN FIGURINES—ONE, A GUARDSMAN ABOUT
TO BLOW A TRUMPET. THE TRUMPET DID NOT BLOW, BUT
LOOKED IMPRESSIVE. THE OTHER, A BEARDED FIGURE
AFFECTIONATELY KNOWN AS ROHRAFFE, HELD NO
TRUMPET BUT HAD A VOICE, PROVIDED BY A MAN HIDDEN
IN AN INNER CUBICLE BETWEEN THE FIGURES. THIS
PERSON COULD ALSO MOVE THE ARMS, HEAD AND
MOUTH OF THE MARIONETTE.

Rohraffe

The Clergy took sides, and the Protesters took new names,
and the Alchemists were above it all and vanished.
We think it was the Guilds that brought in Rohraffe
for people had been impatient to get their *say* in
and Rohraffe could utter the plainest of everyday maxims
from out of his wooden mouth to attract attention.
Whatever Rohraffe said was considered magic.
He also sometimes sang with the High Mass Chorus:
The music went up to God while the singers swallowed.
A famous preacher, Geiler of Kaiserberg, brought
a matter into court regarding Rohraffe. He had said
that Geiler's sermons were too long—laden with
Romanized words that confused the issues.
A delicate matter arose when rival Guildsmen
hired Rohraffe to expound on various vintages.
More followed, praising brandies in new-made bottles.
Most daring of the factions went too far,
Proclaiming some wines holier than others.
This brought up a certain wedding where Mother Mary
had said of a family, "They have no wine."
Nobody wished to descend from that impoverishment.
Rohraffe was stopped. And soon gone—like the Alchemists.

Yet the wine was round in its cup, that day in Cana.
On the ground, the shadow and sun were interchangeable:
a wine both white and clear, without sponsor or price.

A NOTE TO TOURISTS: DON'T GET OFF THE BUS AT GUTENBERG PLAZA IN STRASBOURG. TAKE A TAXI TO A PLACE THAT DOESN'T EXIST, OR SO THE TOWN CHAMBER OF COMMERCE TELLS YOU, OR ANY CONCIERGE OF ANY HOTEL. FIND IT YOURSELF IN SOMEBODY'S BACK YARD. THEY WILL SIMPLY SAY, "OVER THAT PATH . . . ACROSS THE RIVER. YOU'LL FIND IT THERE."

The Gutenberg Island Monument
Near Green Mountain

In 1893, in order to preserve the memory of the invention of printing, a pillar was erected on a small island, near the place where the Convent St. Arbogast stood in the old days. That island was called *Coleo*, pseudonym for Ferdinand Reiber, its owner, who bequeathed it to the city of Strasbourg. The inscription on the surface of the stone was translated from German into French in 1926. It reads:

"Here, at Green Mountain, John Gutenberg discovered printing and through it light spread all over the world."

In the old times, on the 24th of June (St. John's Day) printers and typesetters used to go to the place on pilgrimage.

— Translated from the French
by Mrs. Jacqueline de Fargues
Bibliotheque Municipale
3 rue Kuhn
67000 Strasbourg
France

The Gutenberg Statue at Gutenberg Square

SELECTED BIBLIOGRAPHY

The Coming of the Book by Lucien Febvre, translated from the French by Henri-Jean Martin. Verso Editions, 1984; ISBN 0-86091-797-5. Obtainable through Foyles, London.

Johann Gutenberg and His Bible by Janet Ing. Recommended to me by Joyce Lancaster Wilson, an outstanding scholar regarding printing. This, as well as the reference on Caxton, is a short pamphlet.

Gutenberg & the Beginnings of Print at Mainz, obtained from the Gutenberg Museum at Mainz. Translated from the German by Dr. Charles McCoy, Professor on the staff of the Graduate Theological Union, Pacific School of Religion, Berkeley, CA.

The Strasbourg Documents, I read and had much copied at U.C. Berkeley (the library of the school for librarians) and also at the Huntington Library, Pasadena.

The Lincoln Caxton by Naomi Pearman, Lincoln Cathedral Publications, Lincoln, England.

Many reference books for special subjects such as:

Effect of Printing on the Culture of the West by Elizabeth Eisenstein.

500 Years of Printing by S.H. Steinberg, Penguin Books.

Computers and the Human Mind Donald G. Fink, Anchor Books, N.Y.

Encyclopedia Britannica on Gutenberg, Charlemagne, Troubadours.

Gutenberg and the Beginnings of Print at Strasbourg, archives of the Bibliotheque Municipale de Strasbourg. In French.

RESEARCH AND COMMENTS

Research for the work was done at the University of California at Berkeley (Doe Library of the Education School), at the Huntington Library in Pasadena, and the Gutenberg Museum at Mainz, Germany. I also visited the Bibliotheque Nationale in Paris where I was assisted by Marie Laure Merveille, scholar and translator of French and Latin manuscripts. Most of the libraries mentioned had either originals or copies of the Gutenberg Bible.

I also had the assistance of Dr. Charles McCoy, Robert Gordon Sproul Professor at the Pacific School of Religion in Berkeley, in translating material in German from the Mainz Museum. The Department of Ancient Documents in Strasbourg was cooperative, as was the Bibliotheque Municipale in Strasbourg.

Some records about the Gensfleisch family exist in Mainz, but much was destroyed by fire both in that city as well as in Strasbourg. Remaining is a collection called THE STRASBOURG DOCUMENTS, and it is comprised entirely of lawsuits against Gutenberg. The court cases, as I have indicated, were very informal, full of gossip and irrelevant material with many people coming forward as witnesses with hearsay and rumors.

In contrast to the disclaimers in many volumes based on people's lives, all of the names and places indicated in this book are historically true,* although the treatment and detail are fictional, as imagined by the writer. The major events are accurate: the jailing of the Mainz City Treasurer, moving the Press to Andrew's house; his death on Christmas; restrictions as to membership in the Guilds and other cultural factors; the pilgrimage to Aachen and manufacture of mirrors; etc.

— *Rosalie Moore*

* There are a few exceptions:

We have nothing to indicate that Ann was a widow. There is no record of her life at all, except as she exists in the Breach of Promise Suit.

There is some indication that Johann's brother, Freile, may have been a labor organizer. Making him a blacksmith is the writer's invention.

COLOPHON

Printed and bound by McNaughton & Gunn in the fall of 1995. Published in an edition of 1,000 softcover and 150 casebound copies by Floating Island Publications of Cedarville, California. All typography and text preparation by Wordsworth of San Geronimo, California. The typeface for the text is Galliard. Cover mechanical and type by Michael Sykes at Great Basin Books in Cedarville. This is the fifty-first title from Floating Island Publications and next spring the 52nd title, *Conversations With Bigfoot*, will conclude the first twenty years of press publications that began in Point Reyes Station, California in March, 1976 with *Floating Island I*, the first of four anthologies of poetry, fiction, photography and graphic arts that form the hub of a wheel from which all the other books by individual authors radiate.

Selected Titles from
Floating Island Publications

Barn Fires by Peter Wild
Desemboque by Frank Graziano
Sleeping With The Enemy by Christina Zawadiwsky
The Golden Legend by Jeffery Beam
Up My Coast by Joanne Kyger
Penguins by David Hilton
Dazzled by Arthur Sze
The Cowboy from Phantom Banks by John Brandi
Drug Abuse in Marin County by Eugene Lesser
Black Ash, Orange Fire by William Witherup
Flying the Red Eye by Frank Stewart
Point Reyes Poems by Robert Bly
Ordinary Messengers by Michael Hannon
Seminary Poems by Diane di Prima
Park by Cole Swensen
The Raven Wakes Me Up by Stephan Torre
Blue Skies by Robert Fromberg
Ten Poems by Issa, English Versions by Robert Bly
Sheet of Glass by Stefanie Marlis
Cazadero Poems by Susan Kennedy & Mike Tuggle
He Painted Cape Cod by Barbara M'Cready Sykes
Winter Channels by James Schevill
Poetry Is Dangerous by Tony Moffeit
Music by Kirk Robertson
Wild Harvest by Michael Whitt

Floating Island, First Series
   Volumes I–IV